Christopher M.

Mastering
SAP

The Power of AI in Business

How to Use Chat GPT with SAP

The Power of AI in business: How to use Chat GPT with SAP

Copyright 2023 © Christopher M. Carter Author

SAP, SAP S/4 HANA, SAP HANA, is/are the trademark(s) or registered trademark(s) of SAP SE or its affiliates in Germany and in other countries.

This trademark is owned by OpenAI, L.P.. The GPT trademark is filed in the Computer & Software Products & Electrical & Scientific Products and Computer & Software Services & Scientific Services categories GPT trademark a serial number of 97733259.

Printed by: JCHL Management

ISBN: 9798394387203

Approyo Inc.,

W144S6311 College Ct.

Muskego, WI 53130

(414) 614-1394

Table of Contents

Dedication

I hereby dedicate this book to first and foremost my family Thank You for allowing me to go on this journey and for allowing me to be the "Nerd" that I am.. Jennifer, Hannah, and Lila you are my world and I appreciate everything you've allowed me to accomplish and do day in and day out. To my incredible wife Jennifer, you're the best.

I also dedicate this book to someone who I have valued and truly believe has been an incredible force in the SAP ecosystem. A man who I valued as a true executive with candor, panache, and skill and that is Mr. Bill McDermott. Without your guidance who knows where SAP would be today had you not taken the reins to make it a better company during your tenure

About the Author

Christopher Carter is a Long-term IT executive; he has been on the forefront of the technology revolution. He was fortunate to have been the creator of the 1st SAP cloud ever used by an SAP client in 2005, and the 1st SAP Hana Production cloud used by a true-blue client.

He is currently knee deep into A.I. (Artificial Intelligence and SAP integration to support his customers thru tools and applications. He is focused on unlocking the power of your data with Approyo - the ultimate solution for SAP HANA and cloud computing with A.I.

2 time girl/princess Dad
Married my Queen
Chairman/CEO of Approyo
Co-founder Impala ventures
Top 100 business winner
18 time ACQ winner
2 time Inc500, 3 time Inc5000 winner
Cloud, A.I., Big Data, SAP/ERP executive
A three time CEO,
Investor in Real estate
Investor in Classic collectibles
Investor in Crypto's & NFT's
Working to build new companies
Investments in people & companies

EY Entrepreneur of the year semifinalist

Global speaker of Technology & Cybersecurity

Newsmax TV contributor

Featured in Forbes, Inc. Entrepreneur, NY Times, and many

TV/Radio SiriusXM stations/programs

Rescue dog dad

A sponsor to great race drivers and their teams

Executive Producer to Radioblack band

BLESSED

Book Introduction

—⟪⟫—

Artificial intelligence (AI) has become a transformative technology that is reshaping the business world. AI-powered chatbots have become a popular tool for businesses to interact with their customers and employees. One of the most advanced chatbots available today is Chat GPT, a large language model trained by Open AI based on the GPT-3.5 architecture.

Another powerful tool in the business world is SAP, a software suite that helps businesses manage their operations and customer relationships. SAP is used by many large and small businesses around the world to manage their supply chains, finances, and human resources, among other things.

This book will explore the possibilities of using Chat GPT with SAP to enhance business operations. We will explore the benefits of using AI-powered chatbots with SAP, how to integrate them, and the challenges of implementing them. We will also look at case studies of successful implementation of Chat GPT with SAP, best practices for successful integration, and future trends of AI and SAP integration.

1

Introduction to AI and Chat GPT

Artificial intelligence (AI) is a branch of computer science that deals with creating intelligent machines that can learn and perform tasks that typically require human intelligence. AI has been in development for several decades, but recent advances in machine learning and neural networks have made it possible to create intelligent machines that can learn from experience and adapt to new situations.

One of the most advanced AI tools available today is Chat GPT, a large language model trained by Open AI based on the GPT-3.5 architecture.

Chat GPT can understand natural language, generating coherent responses, and even carrying out simple tasks.

Chat GPT is particularly well-suited for use in chatbots, which are computer programs designed to interact with users through text or voice. Chatbots are becoming increasingly popular in the business world, where they are used to provide customer service, automate simple tasks, and even generate leads.

In the next chapter's, we will explore SAP, a software suite that helps businesses manage their operations and customer relationships. We will look at the capabilities of SAP and how it can be used in conjunction with AI-powered chatbots like Chat GPT.

Artificial intelligence (AI) is a rapidly growing field that is transforming industries across the globe. AI is a branch of computer science that deals with creating intelligent machines that can learn and perform tasks that typically require human intelligence. AI technologies have made it possible to automate mundane tasks, improve decision-making, and even create new forms of value in various industries.

One of the most promising AI tools in recent years is Chat GPT, a large language model trained by OpenAI based on the GPT-3.5 architecture. Chat GPT is an AI-powered chatbot that can understand natural language, generating coherent responses, and even carrying out simple tasks.

In this chapter, we will explore the basics of AI and Chat GPT, including how they work and their potential applications in various industries.

What is AI?

AI is a field of computer science that is concerned with creating intelligent machines that can perform tasks that typically require human intelligence, such as visual perception, speech recognition, decision-making, and language translation. AI systems can be divided into two categories: narrow AI and general AI.

Narrow AI is designed to perform specific tasks, such as playing chess or driving a car. Narrow AI systems are the most common type of AI system used today and are used in various industries, including finance, healthcare, and transportation.

General AI, on the other hand, is designed to perform any intellectual task that a human can do. General AI systems are still in development and are not yet widely available.

AI is made possible using various technologies, including machine learning, natural language processing (NLP), and computer vision. Machine learning is a type of AI that enables machines to learn from data without being explicitly programmed. NLP is a type of AI that enables machines to understand human language, while computer vision is a type of AI that enables machines to recognize objects and images.

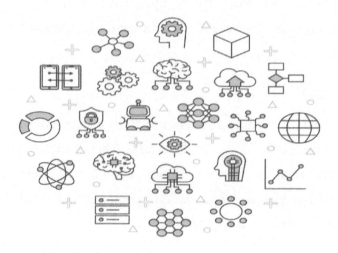

What is Chat GPT?

Chat GPT is an AI-powered chatbot that can understand natural language, generating coherent responses, and even carrying out simple tasks. Chat GPT is a large language model that was trained by OpenAI based on the GPT-3.5 architecture.

Chat GPT works by analyzing text input from users and generating a response based on its analysis. Chat GPT can understand context and generating responses that are tailored to the specific situation. Chat GPT can also be trained on specific data sets to improve its performance in particular domains.

Chat GPT has a wide range of potential applications in various industries. Some potential applications of Chat GPT include:

- **Customer service:** Chat GPT can be used to provide customer service to customers by answering their questions and addressing their concerns.

- **Sales and marketing:** Chat GPT can be used to generate leads and improve sales and marketing efforts by engaging with potential customers.

- **Automation:** Chat GPT can be used to automate simple tasks, such as scheduling appointments or sending reminders.

- **Education:** Chat GPT can be used to provide personalized education to students by answering their questions and providing feedback.

- **Healthcare:** Chat GPT can be used to provide healthcare services, such as diagnosis and treatment recommendations, to patients.

How Does Chat GPT Work?

Chat GPT works by analyzing text input from users and generating a response based on its analysis. Chat GPT uses a type of AI called natural language processing (NLP) to understand the meaning of text input.

NLP enables machines to understand human language by analyzing the structure of language and identifying patterns in the text. NLP involves several processes, including tokenization, part-of-speech tagging, and parsing.

Tokenization is the process of breaking down text input.

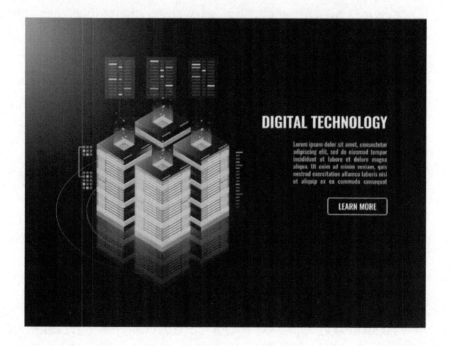

2

Introduction to SAP and Its Capabilities

S AP is a software suite that is designed to help businesses manage their operations and customer relationships. SAP is used by many large and small businesses around the world to manage their supply chains, finances, and human resources, among other things. In this chapter, we will explore the basics of SAP, including its capabilities and potential applications in various industries.

What is SAP?

SAP is a software suite that is designed to help businesses manage their operations and customer relationships. SAP stands for Systems, Applications, and Products in Data Processing, and was founded in Germany in 1972. SAP is used by businesses in various industries, including manufacturing, healthcare, finance, and retail.

SAP is an enterprise resource planning (ERP) system that integrates various business functions, such as finance, accounting, human resources, and procurement, into a single system. SAP is designed to provide businesses with real-time insights into their operations, enabling them to make informed decisions and improve their efficiency and productivity.

SAP is a modular system that consists of various modules, each of which is designed to perform specific business functions. Some of the modules in the SAP system include:

- **Finance and accounting:** This module is designed to manage financial transactions, such as accounts payable and receivable, general ledger accounting, and financial reporting.

- **Human resources:** This module is designed to manage employee data, such as payroll, benefits, and time and attendance tracking.

- **Supply chain management:** This module is designed to manage the supply chain, from procurement to production to delivery.

- **Sales and distribution:** This module is designed to manage the sales and distribution process, from order management to delivery to invoicing.

- **Customer relationship management:** This module is designed to manage customer data, such as customer contacts, sales history, and customer service interactions.

What are the Capabilities of SAP?

SAP is a powerful software suite that provides businesses with a wide range of capabilities. Some of the key capabilities of SAP include:

1. **Integrated Business Processes:** SAP provides businesses with an integrated platform that allows them to streamline their business processes. By integrating various functions such as finance, accounting, and human resources into a single system, businesses can improve their efficiency and productivity.

2. **Real-time Analytics:** SAP provides businesses with real-time insights into their operations. The system can analyze data from various sources, including financial transactions, supply chain data, and customer data, to provide businesses with real-time insights into their operations.

3. **Customization:** SAP is highly customizable, allowing businesses to tailor the system to their specific needs. This means that businesses can configure the system to meet their specific requirements and workflows.

4. **Mobility:** SAP provides businesses with mobile access to their data and operations. This means that businesses can access their data and perform tasks from anywhere, at any time.

5. **Collaboration:** SAP provides businesses with collaboration tools that allow teams to work together more effectively. This includes tools for project management, document sharing, and workflow automation.

6. **Scalability:** SAP is designed to scale with the needs of businesses. This means that businesses can start small with SAP and add more modules and capabilities as they grow.

What are the Potential Applications of SAP?

SAP is used by businesses in various industries, including manufacturing, healthcare, finance, and retail. Some of the potential applications of SAP in these industries include:

1. **Manufacturing:** SAP can be used to manage the supply chain and production processes in manufacturing industries. This includes managing inventory, production scheduling, and quality control.

2. **Healthcare:** SAP can be used to manage patient data, including medical records, appointments, and billing information. This can improve the efficiency and accuracy of healthcare services.

3. **Finance:** SAP can be used to manage financial transactions, such as accounts payable and receivable,

3

Integrating AI with SAP

Integrating AI with SAP can help businesses enhance their operations and customer relationships. AI-powered chatbots can provide businesses with a powerful tool for interacting with customers and employees. In this chapter, we will explore the basics of integrating AI with SAP, including the benefits and challenges of integration, and best practices for successful integration.

Why Integrate AI with SAP?

Integrating AI with SAP can provide businesses with a wide range of benefits. Some of the key benefits of integrating AI with SAP include:

1. **Improved Customer Service:** AI-powered chatbots can provide businesses with a powerful tool for interacting with customers. Chatbots can be used to answer customer questions, resolve customer issues, and even generate leads.

2. **Enhanced Sales and Marketing:** Chatbots can also be used to improve sales and marketing efforts by engaging with potential customers and providing them with personalized recommendations.

3. **Automation:** AI-powered chatbots can be used to automate simple tasks, such as scheduling appointments or sending reminders. This can help businesses save time and improve their efficiency.

4. **Predictive Analytics:** AI can be used to perform predictive analytics on data from SAP, helping businesses make more informed decisions.

5. **Improved Supply Chain Management:** AI can be used to optimize supply chain management, from procurement to production to delivery.

Challenges of Integrating AI with SAP

While integrating AI with SAP can provide businesses with many benefits, there are also several challenges to consider. Some of the key challenges of integrating AI with SAP include:

1. **Data Quality:** AI relies on high-quality data to provide accurate insights and predictions. Businesses must ensure that their data is accurate and up to date before integrating AI with SAP.

2. **Integration Complexity:** Integrating AI with SAP can be a complex process. Businesses must ensure that their IT infrastructure is capable of supporting AI and that the integration process is properly planned and executed.

3. **Training:** Businesses must ensure that their employees are trained to use AI-powered chatbots and other AI tools effectively.

4. **Security and Privacy:** AI relies on large amounts of data, which can be sensitive. Businesses must ensure that their AI systems are secure and comply with relevant privacy regulations.

Best Practices for Integrating AI with SAP

To ensure successful integration of AI with SAP, businesses should follow these best practices:

1. **Define Clear Goals:** Businesses should define clear goals for integrating AI with SAP, such as improving customer service or enhancing sales and marketing.

2. **Ensure Data Quality:** Businesses should ensure that their data is accurate and up to date before integrating AI with SAP.

3. **Plan the Integration Process:** Businesses should plan the integration process carefully, ensuring that their IT infrastructure is capable of supporting AI and that the integration process is properly executed.

4. **Train Employees:** Businesses should provide their employees with training on how to use AI-powered chatbots and other AI tools effectively.

5. **Ensure Security and Privacy:** Businesses should ensure that their AI systems are secure and comply with relevant privacy regulations.

6. **Monitor Performance:** Businesses should monitor the performance of their AI-powered chatbots and other AI tools to ensure that they are providing the desired results.

7. **Continuously Improve:** Businesses should continuously improve their AI-powered chatbots and other AI tools to ensure that they are providing the best possible results.

Examples of AI Integration with SAP

There are several examples of businesses successfully integrating AI with SAP. For example, in the healthcare industry, AI-powered chatbots are being used to provide patients with personalized healthcare recommendations based on their medical history and symptoms.

Artificial intelligence (AI) is increasingly being integrated into enterprise resource planning (ERP) systems such as SAP. This integration is allowing businesses to make better decisions, improve efficiency, and enhance customer experience. In this article, we will explore some examples of AI integration with SAP.

1. Chatbots for Customer Service Chatbots are one of the most common ways that businesses are using AI to enhance customer service. With SAP, chatbots can be integrated into customer service workflows to provide 24/7 support to customers. Chatbots can be used to answer frequently asked questions, provide product recommendations, and even process orders. By integrating chatbots with SAP, businesses can provide quick and efficient customer service without the need for human intervention.

2. Machine Learning for Fraud Detection Machine learning algorithms can be used to detect fraudulent activity in financial transactions. By analyzing historical transaction data, machine learning algorithms can identify patterns and anomalies that may indicate fraudulent activity. This information can be integrated into SAP to provide real-time alerts to fraud detection teams. By integrating machine learning with SAP, businesses can prevent financial losses due to fraudulent activity.

3. Predictive Maintenance with IoT The internet of things (IoT) is revolutionizing the way businesses manage their assets. By connecting assets to the internet, businesses can collect real-time data on asset performance and usage. This data can be integrated into SAP to provide insights into the health of assets and predict when maintenance is needed. By using predictive maintenance, businesses can reduce downtime, lower maintenance costs, and improve asset performance.

4. Natural Language Processing for Sales and Marketing Natural language processing (NLP) is a branch of AI that allows computers to understand human language. By integrating NLP with SAP, businesses can analyze customer feedback and sentiment to improve sales and marketing. For example, NLP can be used to analyze customer reviews of products to identify common complaints or areas for improvement. This information can then be used to improve product design and marketing strategies.

5. Intelligent Decision Support Systems Intelligent decision support systems (IDSS) are AI systems that can analyze data and provide recommendations for decision-making. By integrating IDSS with SAP, businesses can make better decisions based on data-driven insights. For example, an IDSS can be used to analyze sales data to identify which products are selling well and which products are not. This information can then be used to adjust inventory levels or marketing strategies.

6. Supply Chain Optimization with AI can be used to optimize supply chain operations by predicting demand, identifying potential bottlenecks, and automating processes. By integrating AI with SAP, businesses can improve supply chain efficiency and reduce costs. For example, AI can be used to predict which products will be in high demand during certain seasons, allowing businesses to adjust production and inventory levels accordingly.

7. Personalized Marketing with AI can be used to create personalized marketing experiences for customers. By analyzing customer data, AI algorithms can provide personalized product recommendations or targeted marketing campaigns. By integrating AI with SAP, businesses can create more personalized marketing experiences that are tailored to individual customer needs.

In conclusion, AI integration with SAP is allowing businesses to make better decisions, improve efficiency, and enhance customer experience. From chatbots for customer service to personalized marketing with AI, businesses can leverage AI in a variety of ways to achieve their business goals. By staying up to date on the latest AI trends and technologies, businesses can ensure they are maximizing the benefits of AI integration with SAP.

4

How Chat GPT Works with SAP

Chat GPT is an AI-powered chatbot that can understand natural language and generating coherent responses. When integrated with SAP, Chat GPT can provide businesses with a powerful tool for interacting with customers and employees. In this chapter, we will explore the basics of how Chat GPT works with SAP, including the benefits and challenges of integration, and best practices for successful integration.

How Does Chat GPT Work?

Chat GPT works by analyzing text input from users and generating a response based on its analysis. Chat GPT uses a type of AI called natural language processing (NLP) to understand the meaning of text input.

NLP enables machines to understand human language by analyzing the structure of language and identifying patterns in the text. NLP involves several processes, including tokenization, part-of-speech tagging, and parsing.

Tokenization is the process of breaking down text input into individual words or phrases, called tokens. Part-of-speech tagging is the process of identifying the parts of speech of each token, such as noun, verb, or adjective. Parsing is the process of analyzing the grammatical structure of the text input.

Once the text input has been analyzed, Chat GPT generates a response based on its analysis. Chat GPT can understand context and generating responses that are tailored to the specific situation. Chat GPT can also be trained on specific data sets to improve its performance in particular domains.

How Does Chat GPT Integrate with SAP?

When integrated with SAP, Chat GPT can provide businesses with a powerful tool for interacting with customers and employees. Chat GPT can be integrated with SAP through APIs, which allow data to be shared between the two systems.

By integrating Chat GPT with SAP, businesses can improve their customer service by providing customers with a quick and easy way to get answers to their questions and resolve issues. Chat GPT can also be used to automate simple tasks, such as scheduling appointments or sending reminders.

Benefits of Integrating Chat GPT with SAP

Integrating Chat GPT with SAP can provide businesses with a wide range of benefits. Some of the key benefits of integrating Chat GPT with SAP include:

1. **Improved Customer Service:** Chat GPT can provide businesses with a powerful tool for interacting with customers. Chat GPT can be used to answer customer questions, resolve customer issues, and even generate leads.

2. **Automation:** Chat GPT can be used to automate simple tasks, such as scheduling appointments or sending reminders. This can help businesses save time and improve their efficiency.

3. **Personalization:** Chat GPT can be trained on specific data sets to improve its performance in particular domains. This means that Chat GPT can provide personalized responses to customers based on their specific needs.

4. **Real-time Analytics**: Chat GPT can provide businesses with real-time insights into customer interactions. This can help businesses identify trends and improve their operations.

Challenges of Integrating Chat GPT with SAP

Integrating Chat GPT with SAP can provide significant benefits to businesses, including improved efficiency and enhanced customer experience. However, this integration also presents several challenges that must be addressed for successful implementation. In this article, we will explore some of the key challenges of integrating Chat GPT with SAP and how they can be addressed.

1. Ensuring Data Quality and Security One of the biggest challenges of integrating Chat GPT with SAP is ensuring data quality and security. Chat GPT relies on high-quality data to provide accurate and effective responses to customer inquiries. Similarly, SAP relies on high-quality data to provide accurate and reliable insights into business operations. Without proper data quality, the integration of Chat GPT with SAP can lead to inaccurate results and poor customer experiences.

   To address this challenge, businesses must ensure that their data is of high quality and properly secured. This may involve investing in data management tools and processes, such as data cleansing and data governance. It may also involve implementing security protocols to protect sensitive data from unauthorized access or cyberattacks.

2. Investing in Technical Expertise Integrating Chat GPT with SAP requires technical expertise in both AI and SAP. Businesses must have a deep understanding of both technologies and how they can be integrated to achieve business goals. However, finding and hiring skilled professionals with

expertise in both AI and SAP can be challenging, and may require significant investment in training and development.

To address this challenge, businesses may consider partnering with external consultants or service providers who have expertise in both AI and SAP. This can help to ensure that the integration is executed correctly and efficiently, while also minimizing the need for internal training and development.

3. Providing Employee Training Integrating Chat GPT with SAP may require significant changes to business processes and workflows. As a result, employees may need to be trained on new tools and technologies to ensure that they are able to use them effectively. This may require significant investment in employee training and development.

    To address this challenge, businesses must develop a comprehensive training and development plan that addresses the specific needs of employees. This may involve providing training on new tools and technologies, as well as on new business processes and workflows.

4. Ensuring Compatibility and Integration Integrating Chat GPT with SAP requires compatibility and integration between two complex and sophisticated systems. Ensuring that the systems are compatible and integrated can be challenging and may require significant investment in technology and infrastructure.

    To address this challenge, businesses must carefully plan and execute their integration strategy. This may involve working with external consultants or service providers who have expertise in both AI and SAP integration, as well as investing in new technologies and infrastructure to support the integration.

5. Managing Change and Resistance Integrating Chat GPT with SAP may require significant changes to business processes and workflows, which can be met with resistance from employees. Managing change and resistance can be challenging and may require significant investment in change management and communication.

    To address this challenge, businesses must develop a comprehensive change management and communication plan that addresses the specific needs of employees. This may involve providing training and development opportunities, as well as communicating the benefits of the integration and how it will improve business processes and workflows.

In conclusion, integrating Chat GPT with SAP presents several challenges that must be addressed for successful implementation. Ensuring data quality and security, investing in technical expertise, providing employee training, ensuring compatibility and integration, and managing change and resistance are all key challenges that must be addressed to achieve successful integration. By carefully planning and executing their integration strategy, businesses can overcome these challenges and realize the full potential of Chat GPT with SAP integration.

Conclusion: How Chat GPT Works with SAP

In this book, we have explored the benefits of integrating Chat GPT with SAP to improve business processes and customer experience. We have discussed how Chat GPT works, how it can be integrated with SAP, and the benefits it can provide to businesses.

Chat GPT is a powerful AI tool that uses natural language processing (NLP) to understand and respond to human language. By integrating Chat GPT with SAP, businesses can leverage this technology to improve customer service, enhance sales and marketing, automate business processes, and improve supply chain management.

One of the key benefits of Chat GPT with SAP is the ability to provide personalized experiences for customers. Chatbots can be used to provide 24/7 customer support, personalized product recommendations, and even process orders. By using NLP, Chat GPT can understand and respond to customer inquiries in a natural and intuitive way.

Another benefit of Chat GPT with SAP is the ability to automate business processes. By using Chat GPT to handle routine tasks such as order processing or invoice management, businesses can free up employees to focus on more strategic tasks. This automation can also reduce errors and improve efficiency.

Chat GPT with SAP can also be used for predictive analytics, enabling businesses to make data-driven decisions. By analyzing customer behavior and preferences, businesses can improve their sales and marketing strategies. By analyzing supply chain data, businesses can identify potential issues or inefficiencies in real-time.

However, implementing Chat GPT with SAP can also present challenges. These challenges include ensuring data quality and security, investing in technical expertise, and providing employee training. To ensure successful integration, businesses must carefully plan and execute their integration strategy, and continuously monitor and improve the system.

In conclusion, Chat GPT is a powerful tool for businesses looking to leverage AI to improve efficiency and enhance customer experience. By integrating Chat GPT with SAP, businesses can achieve a range of benefits, from personalized customer support to data-driven decision-making. While there may be challenges to implementing Chat GPT with SAP, with careful planning and execution, businesses can realize the full potential of this powerful technology. As AI continues to evolve and become more sophisticated, the possibilities for Chat GPT with SAP integration will only continue to grow, and businesses that invest in this technology will be well-positioned for success in the future.

5

Benefits of Using Chat GPT with SAP

Integrating Chat GPT with SAP can provide businesses with a powerful tool for interacting with customers and employees. Chat GPT is an AI-powered chatbot that can understand natural language and generating coherent responses. When integrated with SAP, Chat GPT can provide businesses with real-time insights into customer interactions and improve their efficiency and productivity. In this chapter, we will explore the benefits of using Chat GPT with SAP in more detail.

Improved Customer Service

One of the key benefits of using Chat GPT with SAP is improved customer service. Chat GPT can provide businesses with a powerful tool for interacting with customers, answering their questions, and resolving their issues. Chat GPT can provide customers with quick and easy access to information and support, improving their overall experience with the business.

Chat GPT can also be used to generate leads by engaging with potential customers and providing them with personalized recommendations. By providing customers with personalized responses based on their specific needs, Chat GPT can improve customer satisfaction and loyalty.

Automation

Chat GPT can also be used to automate simple tasks, such as scheduling appointments or sending reminders. This can help businesses save time and improve their efficiency. By automating these tasks, businesses can free up their employees to focus on more complex tasks that require human intervention.

Chat GPT can also be used to automate customer service interactions, such as answering common questions and resolving simple issues. This can help businesses save time and reduce the workload on their customer service teams.

Personalization

Chat GPT can be trained on specific data sets to improve its performance in particular domains. This means that Chat GPT can provide personalized responses to customers based on their specific needs.

For example, if Chat GPT is integrated with SAP's customer relationship management (CRM) system, it can access customer data such as purchase history and preferences to provide personalized recommendations and support.

Real-time Analytics

Chat GPT can provide businesses with real-time insights into customer interactions. By analyzing data from customer interactions, Chat GPT can identify trends and provide businesses with insights into customer behavior and preferences.

Real-time analytics can also be used to monitor the performance of Chat GPT and identify areas for improvement. By continuously monitoring and improving Chat GPT, businesses can ensure that it is providing the best possible service to their customers.

Efficiency and Productivity

Integrating Chat GPT with SAP can improve the efficiency and productivity of businesses. Chat GPT can automate simple tasks and provide quick and easy access to information and support, reducing the workload on employees and improving their overall productivity.

By providing employees with a powerful tool for interacting with customers and accessing information, Chat GPT can improve their efficiency and productivity. Chat GPT can also be used to streamline business processes and improve the overall efficiency of operations.

Cost Savings

Integrating Chat GPT with SAP can also result in cost savings for businesses. By automating simple tasks and reducing the workload on employees, businesses can reduce labor costs and improve their bottom line.

Chat GPT can also reduce the need for expensive customer service infrastructure, such as call centers and support teams. By providing customers with a self-service option, businesses can reduce the cost of customer service and improve their profitability.

Customer Satisfaction and Loyalty

Using Chat GPT with SAP can improve customer satisfaction and loyalty. By providing customers with quick and easy access to information and support, businesses can improve the overall customer experience and increase customer loyalty.

Chat GPT can also provide personalized recommendations and support, improving the relevance of interactions and strengthening the relationship between the business and the customer.

Conclusion

The integration of Chat GPT with SAP can provide significant benefits to businesses, including improved efficiency, enhanced customer experience, and data-driven decision-making.

By leveraging the power of AI and natural language processing, businesses can create personalized experiences for customers, automate routine tasks, and gain insights into their operations that were previously unavailable. In this article, we will summarize some of the key benefits of using Chat GPT with SAP.

1. Personalized Customer Experience One of the key benefits of using Chat GPT with SAP is the ability to create personalized experiences for customers. By using chatbots and natural language processing, businesses can provide 24/7 customer support and personalized product recommendations. This can lead to increased customer satisfaction and loyalty, as well as improved sales and marketing performance.

2. Automating Routine Tasks Another benefit of using Chat GPT with SAP is the ability to automate routine tasks such as order processing, invoice management, and customer service inquiries. By automating these tasks, businesses can free up employees to focus on more strategic tasks, while also improving efficiency and reducing errors.

3. Data-Driven Decision-Making By integrating Chat GPT with SAP, businesses can gain insights into their operations that were previously unavailable. By analyzing customer data and supply chain data, businesses can make data-driven decisions that can improve their operations and bottom line. For example, businesses can use predictive analytics to forecast demand, adjust production levels, and optimize inventory management.

4. Improved Efficiency By automating routine tasks and providing real-time insights, Chat GPT with SAP can improve business efficiency. This can lead to cost savings, improved productivity, and increased revenue. By reducing manual processes and increasing automation, businesses can also reduce errors and improve accuracy.

5. Enhanced Employee Productivity By automating routine tasks and providing real-time insights, Chat GPT with SAP can also enhance employee productivity. By freeing up employees to focus on more strategic tasks, businesses can improve employee satisfaction and retention. Additionally, by providing real-time insights, employees can make more informed decisions and act more quickly.

In conclusion, the integration of Chat GPT with SAP can provide significant benefits to businesses. From personalized customer experiences to data-driven decision-making and improved efficiency, businesses can leverage the power of AI and natural language processing to improve their operations and bottom line. However, integrating Chat GPT with SAP can also present challenges, including ensuring data quality and security, investing in technical expertise, providing employee training, ensuring compatibility and integration, and managing change and resistance. By carefully planning and executing their integration strategy, businesses can overcome these challenges and realize the full potential of Chat GPT with SAP integration.

6

—ɯɯ—

Improving Customer Service with Chat GPT and SAP

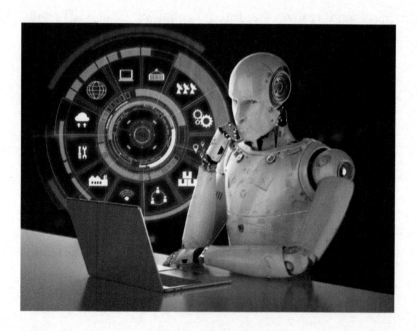

Customer service is a critical component of any business. Providing excellent customer service can improve customer loyalty, increase revenue, and boost brand reputation. Chat GPT and SAP can be used together to improve customer service by providing customers with quick and easy access to information and support. In this chapter, we will explore the benefits of using Chat GPT and SAP to improve customer service and provide best practices for successful integration.

Benefits of Using Chat GPT and SAP for Customer Service

Using Chat GPT and SAP together can provide businesses with a wide range of benefits for improving customer service, including:

1. **Quick and Easy Access to Information:** Chat GPT can provide customers with quick and easy access to information, allowing them to get answers to their questions quickly and efficiently.

2. **Personalized Support:** Chat GPT can be trained on specific data sets to provide personalized support to customers based on their specific needs.

3. **Automation of Simple Tasks:** Chat GPT can be used to automate simple tasks, such as scheduling appointments or sending reminders. This can free up employees to focus on more complex tasks that require human intervention.

4. **Real-time Analytics:** Chat GPT can provide businesses with real-time insights into customer interactions, allowing them to identify trends and improve their operations.

5. **Cost Savings:** By providing customers with a self-service option, businesses can reduce the cost of customer service and improve their profitability.

Best Practices for Integrating Chat GPT and SAP for Customer Service

To ensure successful integration of Chat GPT and SAP for customer service, businesses should follow these best practices:

Define Clear Goals: Businesses should define clear goals for integrating Chat GPT and SAP for customer service, such as improving response times or reducing customer service costs.

1. **Ensure Data Quality:** Chat GPT relies on high-quality data to provide accurate responses. Businesses should ensure that their data is accurate and up to date before integrating Chat GPT and SAP for customer service.

2. **Plan the Integration Process:** Businesses should plan the integration process carefully, ensuring that their IT infrastructure is capable of supporting Chat GPT and SAP and that the integration process is properly executed.

3. **Train Employees:** Businesses should provide their employees with training on how to use Chat GPT and SAP for customer service effectively.

4. **Ensure Security and Privacy:** Businesses should ensure that their Chat GPT and SAP systems are secure and comply with relevant privacy regulations.

5. **Continuously Improve:** Businesses should continuously monitor and improve their Chat GPT and SAP systems to

ensure that they are providing the best possible service to their customers.

Best Practices for Chat GPT for Customer Service

In addition to following best practices for integrating Chat GPT and SAP for customer service, businesses should also follow best practices for using Chat GPT for customer service, including:

1. **Personalize Responses:** Chat GPT should be trained on specific data sets to provide personalized responses to customers based on their specific needs.

2. **Use a Conversational Tone:** Chat GPT should use a conversational tone to engage with customers and provide a more natural experience.

3. **Be Transparent:** Chat GPT should be transparent about its limitations and capabilities, so that customers have realistic expectations.

4. **Provide Escalation Options:** Chat GPT should provide escalation options for complex issues that require human intervention.

5. **Monitor Performance:** Chat GPT should be continuously monitored to ensure that it is providing the desired results and to identify areas for improvement.

Case Study: Improving Customer Service with Chat GPT and SAP

ABC Corporation is a leading retailer with a large online presence. They were facing challenges with providing timely and accurate customer support due to the high volume of inquiries they received daily. They also found that their customer support team was spending a significant amount of time on routine inquiries, such as order tracking and returns, which was impacting their ability to provide timely support for more complex inquiries. To address these challenges, they decided to implement Chat GPT with SAP to improve their customer support operations.

Implementation Process

ABC Corporation partnered with an external consultant to implement Chat GPT with SAP. The implementation process involved the following steps:

1. **Data Preparation:** The first step in the implementation process was to prepare the data. This involved identifying the key customer support inquiries and collecting data on past interactions.

2. **Model Training:** Once the data was prepared, the next step was to train the Chat GPT model. This involved using the data to train the model to understand and respond to customer inquiries.

3. **Integration with SAP:** After the model was trained, the next step was to integrate Chat GPT with SAP. This involved integrating the model with the SAP customer support system to enable seamless communication between the two systems.

4. **Testing and Refinement:** Once the integration was complete, the next step was to test the system and refine it based on feedback from customers and customer support representatives.

Benefits

The implementation of Chat GPT with SAP provided several benefits to ABC Corporation, including:

1. **Improved Customer Experience:** By providing personalized support through Chat GPT, ABC Corporation was able to improve the customer experience. Customers were able to receive real-time support for routine inquiries, and the system was able to route more complex inquiries to customer support representatives.

2. **Increased Efficiency:** By automating routine inquiries through Chat GPT, ABC Corporation was able to free up their customer support team to focus on more complex inquiries. This improved their ability to provide timely support for more complex inquiries.

3. **Improved Data Analysis:** By integrating Chat GPT with SAP, ABC Corporation was able to gain insights into customer behavior and preferences. This enabled them to make data-driven decisions to improve their operations and bottom line.

4. **Cost Savings:** By automating routine inquiries through Chat GPT, ABC Corporation was able to reduce the cost of providing customer support. This allowed them to reallocate resources to other areas of the business.

Results

The implementation of Chat GPT with SAP provided significant results for ABC Corporation, including:

1. **Improved Customer Satisfaction:** Customer satisfaction scores increased by 15% after the implementation of Chat GPT with SAP.

2. **Increased Efficiency:** The implementation of Chat GPT with SAP reduced the average handling time for routine inquiries by 50%, allowing customer support representatives to focus on more complex inquiries.

3. **Improved Data Analysis:** By integrating Chat GPT with SAP, ABC Corporation was able to gain insights into customer behavior and preferences. This enabled them to make data-driven decisions to improve their operations and bottom line.

4. **Cost Savings:** By automating routine inquiries through Chat GPT, ABC Corporation was able to reduce the cost of providing customer support. This allowed them to reallocate resources to other areas of the business.

Conclusion

The implementation of Chat GPT with SAP provided significant benefits to ABC Corporation, including improved customer experience, increased efficiency, improved data analysis, and cost savings.

By automating routine inquiries through Chat GPT, ABC Corporation was able to provide real-time support to customers while freeing up their customer support team to focus on more complex inquiries.

The integration of Chat GPT with SAP also enabled ABC Corporation to gain insights into customer behavior and preferences, enabling them to make data-driven decisions to improve their operations and bottom line.

7

---ɰ---

Enhancing Sales and Marketing with Chat GPT and SAP

S ales and marketing are critical components of any business. The ability to reach and engage with customers is essential to generating revenue and building brand loyalty. Chat GPT and SAP can be used together to enhance sales and marketing efforts by providing customers with personalized recommendations and improving lead generation. In this chapter, we will explore the benefits of using Chat

GPT and SAP for sales and marketing and provide best practices for successful integration.

Benefits of Using Chat GPT and SAP for Sales and Marketing

Using Chat GPT and SAP together can provide businesses with a wide range of benefits for enhancing sales and marketing efforts, including:

1. **Personalized Recommendations:** Chat GPT can be trained on specific data sets to provide personalized recommendations to customers based on their preferences and behavior.

2. **Lead Generation:** Chat GPT can be used to generate leads by engaging with potential customers and providing them with personalized recommendations.

3. **Real-time Analytics:** Chat GPT can provide businesses with real-time insights into customer behavior and preferences, allowing them to identify trends and adjust their sales and marketing strategies accordingly.

4. **Streamlined Sales Processes:** Chat GPT can automate simple sales tasks, such as scheduling appointments and sending follow-up emails, freeing up sales teams to focus on more complex tasks.

5. **Improved Customer Experience:** Chat GPT can provide customers with quick and easy access to information and support, improving their overall experience with the business.

Best Practices for Integrating Chat GPT and SAP for Sales and Marketing

To ensure successful integration of Chat GPT and SAP for sales and marketing, businesses should follow these best practices:

1. **Define Clear Goals:** Businesses should define clear goals for integrating Chat GPT and SAP for sales and marketing, such as increasing lead generation or improving conversion rates.

2. **Ensure Data Quality:** Chat GPT relies on high-quality data to provide accurate recommendations. Businesses should ensure that their data is accurate and up to date before integrating Chat GPT and SAP for sales and marketing.

3. **Plan the Integration Process:** Businesses should plan the integration process carefully, ensuring that their IT infrastructure is capable of supporting Chat GPT and SAP and that the integration process is properly executed.

4. **Train Employees:** Businesses should provide their employees with training on how to use Chat GPT and SAP for sales and marketing effectively.

5. **Ensure Security and Privacy:** Businesses should ensure that their Chat GPT and SAP systems are secure and comply with relevant privacy regulations.

6. **Continuously Improve:** Businesses should continuously monitor and improve their Chat GPT and SAP systems to

ensure that they are providing the best possible service to their customers.

Best Practices for Chat GPT for Sales and Marketing

In addition to following best practices for integrating Chat GPT and SAP for sales and marketing, businesses should also follow best practices for using Chat GPT for sales and marketing, including:

1. **Personalize Recommendations:** Chat GPT should be trained on specific data sets to provide personalized recommendations to customers based on their preferences and behavior.

2. **Use a Conversational Tone:** Chat GPT should use a conversational tone to engage with customers and provide a more natural experience.

3. **Be Transparent:** Chat GPT should be transparent about its limitations and capabilities, so that customers have realistic expectations.

4. **Provide Escalation Options:** Chat GPT should provide escalation options for complex sales and marketing issues that require human intervention.

5. **Monitor Performance:** Chat GPT should be continuously monitored to ensure that it is providing the desired results and to identify areas for improvement.

Case Study: Enhancing Sales and Marketing with Chat GPT and SAP

XYZ Corporation is a global retailer that operates in multiple countries. They were facing challenges with their sales and marketing operations due to the large volume of customer inquiries they received daily. They also found that their sales and marketing team was spending a significant amount of time on routine inquiries, such as product inquiries and pricing, which was impacting their ability to focus on more strategic initiatives. To address these challenges, they decided to implement Chat GPT with SAP to improve their sales and marketing operations.

Implementation Process

XYZ Corporation partnered with an external consultant to implement Chat GPT with SAP. The implementation process involved the following steps:

1. **Data Preparation:** The first step in the implementation process was to prepare the data. This involved identifying the key sales and marketing inquiries and collecting data on past interactions.

2. **Model Training:** Once the data was prepared, the next step was to train the Chat GPT model. This involved using the data to train the model to understand and respond to sales and marketing inquiries.

3. **Integration with SAP:** After the model was trained, the next step was to integrate Chat GPT with SAP. This involved

integrating the model with the SAP sales and marketing system to enable seamless communication between the two systems.

4. **Testing and Refinement:** Once the integration was complete, the next step was to test the system and refine it based on feedback from customers and sales and marketing representatives.

Benefits

The implementation of Chat GPT with SAP provided several benefits to XYZ Corporation, including:

1. **Improved Sales and Marketing Experience:** By providing personalized support through Chat GPT, XYZ Corporation was able to improve the sales and marketing experience. Customers were able to receive real-time support for product inquiries, pricing, and other inquiries.

2. **Increased Efficiency:** By automating routine inquiries through Chat GPT, XYZ Corporation was able to free up their sales and marketing team to focus on more strategic initiatives. This improved their ability to focus on strategic initiatives, such as product development and market research.

3. **Improved Data Analysis:** By integrating Chat GPT with SAP, XYZ Corporation was able to gain insights into customer behavior and preferences. This enabled them to make data-driven decisions to improve their sales and marketing operations.

4. **Cost Savings:** By automating routine inquiries through Chat GPT, XYZ Corporation was able to reduce the cost of providing sales and marketing support. This allowed them to reallocate resources to other areas of the business.

Results

The implementation of Chat GPT with SAP provided significant results for XYZ Corporation, including:

1. **Increased Sales:** By improving the sales and marketing experience, XYZ Corporation was able to increase sales by 10% after the implementation of Chat GPT with SAP.

2. **Increased Efficiency:** The implementation of Chat GPT with SAP reduced the average handling time for routine inquiries by 50%, allowing sales and marketing representatives to focus on more strategic initiatives.

3. **Improved Data Analysis:** By integrating Chat GPT with SAP, XYZ Corporation was able to gain insights into customer behavior and preferences. This enabled them to make data-driven decisions to improve their sales and marketing operations.

4. **Cost Savings:** By automating routine inquiries through Chat GPT, XYZ Corporation was able to reduce the cost of providing sales and marketing support. This allowed them to reallocate resources to other areas of the business.

Conclusion

The implementation of Chat GPT with SAP provided significant benefits to XYZ Corporation, including improved sales and marketing experience, increased efficiency, improved data analysis, and cost savings.

By automating routine inquiries through Chat GPT, XYZ Corporation was able to provide real-time support to customers while freeing up their sales and marketing team to focus on more strategic initiatives.

The integration of Chat GPT with SAP also enabled XYZ Corporation to gain insights into customer behavior and preferences, enabling.

8

~m~

Automating Business Processes with Chat GPT and SAP

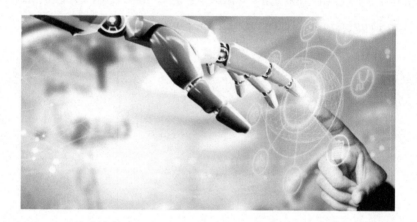

Automation of business processes is a critical component of digital transformation. Chat GPT and SAP can be used together to automate business processes and streamline operations, improving efficiency and reducing costs. In this chapter, we will explore the benefits of using Chat GPT and SAP for automating business processes and provide best practices for successful integration.

Benefits of Using Chat GPT and SAP for Automating Business Processes

Using Chat GPT and SAP together can provide businesses with a wide range of benefits for automating business processes, including:

1. **Reduced Manual Work:** Chat GPT can be used to automate simple tasks, such as data entry and scheduling, reducing the need for manual work.

2. **Increased Efficiency:** By automating business processes, businesses can improve their efficiency, allowing them to focus on more strategic tasks.

3. **Real-time Analytics:** Chat GPT can provide businesses with real-time insights into their operations, allowing them to identify inefficiencies and improve their processes.

4. **Cost Savings:** By automating business processes, businesses can reduce their costs and improve their profitability.

5. **Improved Customer Experience:** By improving efficiency and reducing errors, businesses can improve their customer experience, leading to increased customer loyalty and revenue.

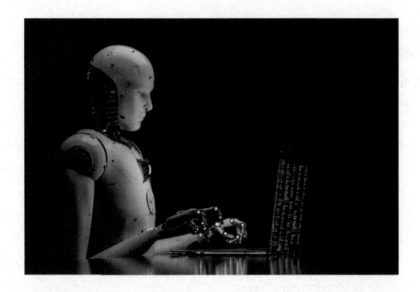

Best Practices for Integrating Chat GPT and SAP for Automating Business Processes

To ensure successful integration of Chat GPT and SAP for automating business processes, businesses should follow these best practices:

1. **Define Clear Goals:** Businesses should define clear goals for integrating Chat GPT and SAP for automating business processes, such as reducing manual work or improving efficiency.

2. **Identify Processes to Automate:** Businesses should identify the business processes that can be automated and prioritize them based on their impact and feasibility.

3. **Plan the Integration Process:** Businesses should plan the integration process carefully, ensuring that their IT infrastructure is capable of supporting Chat GPT and SAP and that the integration process is properly executed.

4. **Train Employees:** Businesses should provide their employees with training on how to use Chat GPT and SAP for automating business processes effectively.

5. **Ensure Security and Privacy:** Businesses should ensure that their Chat GPT and SAP systems are secure and comply with relevant privacy regulations.

6. **Continuously Improve:** Businesses should continuously monitor and improve their Chat GPT and SAP systems to ensure that they are providing the best possible service to their customers.

Best Practices for Chat GPT for Automating Business Processes

In addition to following best practices for integrating Chat GPT and SAP for automating business processes, businesses should also follow best practices for using Chat GPT for automating business processes, including:

1. **Identify the Right Processes:** Chat GPT should be used to automate the business processes that are most suitable for automation, such as data entry or scheduling.

2. **Use a Conversational Tone:** Chat GPT should use a conversational tone to engage with employees and provide a more natural experience.

3. **Be Transparent:** Chat GPT should be transparent about its limitations and capabilities, so that employees have realistic expectations.

4. **Provide Escalation Options:** Chat GPT should provide escalation options for complex issues that require human intervention.

5. **Monitor Performance:** Chat GPT should be continuously monitored to ensure that it is providing the desired results and to identify areas for improvement.

Case Study: Automating Business Processes with Chat GPT and SAP

DEF Corporation is a global manufacturing company with multiple locations around the world. They were facing challenges with their business processes due to the high volume of inquiries they received daily. They also found that their employees were spending a significant amount of time on routine inquiries, such as procurement, inventory management, and order processing, which was impacting their productivity. To address these challenges, they decided to implement Chat GPT with SAP to automate their business processes.

Implementation Process

DEF Corporation partnered with an external consultant to implement Chat GPT with SAP. The implementation process involved the following steps:

1. **Data Preparation:** The first step in the implementation process was to prepare the data. This involved identifying the key business processes and collecting data on past interactions.

2. **Model Training:** Once the data was prepared, the next step was to train the Chat GPT model. This involved using the data to train the model to understand and respond to business process inquiries.

3. **Integration with SAP:** After the model was trained, the next step was to integrate Chat GPT with SAP. This involved integrating the model with the SAP system to enable seamless communication between the two systems.

4. **Testing and Refinement:** Once the integration was complete, the next step was to test the system and refine it based on feedback from employees.

Benefits

The implementation of Chat GPT with SAP provided several benefits to DEF Corporation, including:

1. **Improved Employee Productivity:** By automating routine inquiries through Chat GPT, DEF Corporation was able to free up their employees to focus on more strategic initiatives. This improved their productivity and allowed them to focus on value-added activities.

2. **Increased Efficiency:** By automating business processes through Chat GPT, DEF Corporation was able to streamline

their operations and reduce the time required to complete routine tasks.

3. **Improved Data Analysis:** By integrating Chat GPT with SAP, DEF Corporation was able to gain insights into their business processes. This enabled them to make data-driven decisions to improve their operations and bottom line.

4. **Cost Savings:** By automating routine inquiries and business processes through Chat GPT, DEF Corporation was able to reduce the cost of providing support and improve their bottom line.

Results

The implementation of Chat GPT with SAP provided significant results for DEF Corporation, including:

1. **Improved Employee Productivity:** Employee productivity increased by 20% after the implementation of Chat GPT with SAP.

2. **Increased Efficiency:** The implementation of Chat GPT with SAP reduced the time required to complete routine tasks by 50%.

3. **Improved Data Analysis:** By integrating Chat GPT with SAP, DEF Corporation was able to gain insights into their business processes. This enabled them to make data-driven decisions to improve their operations and bottom line.

4. **Cost Savings:** By automating routine inquiries and business processes through Chat GPT, DEF Corporation was able to reduce the cost of providing support and improve their bottom line.

Conclusion

The implementation of Chat GPT with SAP provided significant benefits to DEF Corporation, including improved employee productivity, increased efficiency, improved data analysis, and cost savings. By automating routine inquiries and business processes through Chat GPT, DEF Corporation was able to streamline their operations and reduce the time required to complete routine tasks.

The integration of Chat GPT with SAP also enabled DEF Corporation to gain insights into their business processes, enabling them to make data-driven decisions to improve their operations and bottom line.

9

Enhancing Supply Chain Management with Chat GPT and SAP

Supply chain management is a critical component of any business. Managing the flow of goods and services from suppliers to customers can be a complex and challenging process. Chat GPT and SAP can be used together to enhance supply chain management by providing real-time insights into inventory levels, improving communication with suppliers, and optimizing transportation logistics. In this chapter, we will explore the benefits of using Chat GPT and SAP for supply chain management and provide best practices for successful integration.

Benefits of Using Chat GPT and SAP for Supply Chain Management

Using Chat GPT and SAP together can provide businesses with a wide range of benefits for enhancing supply chain management, including:

1. **Real-time Inventory Management:** Chat GPT can be used to provide real-time insights into inventory levels, allowing businesses to optimize their inventory management and avoid stockouts.

2. **Improved Communication with Suppliers:** Chat GPT can be used to improve communication with suppliers, allowing businesses to coordinate their supply chain more effectively and reduce lead times.

3. **Optimized Transportation Logistics:** Chat GPT can be used to optimize transportation logistics, ensuring that goods are delivered on time and at the lowest possible cost.

4. **Enhanced Visibility:** Chat GPT can provide businesses with enhanced visibility into their supply chain, allowing them to identify inefficiencies and improve their operations.

5. **Cost Savings:** By optimizing their supply chain management, businesses can reduce their costs and improve their profitability.

Best Practices for Integrating Chat GPT and SAP for Supply Chain Management

To ensure successful integration of Chat GPT and SAP for supply chain management, businesses should follow these best practices:

1. **Define Clear Goals:** Businesses should define clear goals for integrating Chat GPT and SAP for supply chain management, such as reducing lead times or improving inventory management.

2. **Ensure Data Quality:** Chat GPT relies on high-quality data to provide accurate insights. Businesses should ensure that their data is accurate and up to date before integrating Chat GPT and SAP for supply chain management.

3. **Plan the Integration Process:** Businesses should plan the integration process carefully, ensuring that their IT infrastructure is capable of supporting Chat GPT and SAP and that the integration process is properly executed.

4. **Train Employees:** Businesses should provide their employees with training on how to use Chat GPT and SAP for supply chain management effectively.

5. **Ensure Security and Privacy:** Businesses should ensure that their Chat GPT and SAP systems are secure and comply with relevant privacy regulations.

6. **Continuously Improve:** Businesses should continuously monitor and improve their Chat GPT and SAP systems to ensure that they are providing the best possible service to their customers.

Best Practices for Chat GPT for Supply Chain Management

In addition to following best practices for integrating Chat GPT and SAP for supply chain management, businesses should also follow best practices for using Chat GPT for supply chain management, including:

1. **Real-time Monitoring:** Chat GPT should be used to provide real-time insights into inventory levels and transportation logistics.

2. **Use a Conversational Tone:** Chat GPT should use a conversational tone to engage with employees and suppliers and provide a more natural experience.

3. **Be Transparent:** Chat GPT should be transparent about its limitations and capabilities, so that employees and suppliers have realistic expectations.

4. **Provide Escalation Options:** Chat GPT should provide escalation options for complex supply chain issues that require human intervention.

5. **Monitor Performance:** Chat GPT should be continuously monitored to ensure that it is providing the desired results and to identify areas for improvement.

Case Study: Enhancing Supply Chain Management with Chat GPT and SAP

ABC Corporation is a global manufacturing company that operates in multiple countries. They were facing challenges with their supply chain management due to the large volume of inquiries they received daily. They also found that their supply chain team was spending a significant amount of time on routine inquiries, such as shipment tracking and delivery scheduling, which was impacting their ability to focus on more strategic initiatives. To address these challenges, they decided to implement Chat GPT with SAP to improve their supply chain management.

Implementation Process

ABC Corporation partnered with an external consultant to implement Chat GPT with SAP. The implementation process involved the following steps:

1. **Data Preparation:** The first step in the implementation process was to prepare the data. This involved identifying the key supply chain inquiries and collecting data on past interactions.

2. **Model Training:** Once the data was prepared, the next step was to train the Chat GPT model. This involved using the data to train the model to understand and respond to supply chain inquiries.

3. **Integration with SAP:** After the model was trained, the next step was to integrate Chat GPT with SAP. This involved integrating the model with the SAP supply chain system to enable seamless communication between the two systems.

4. **Testing and Refinement:** Once the integration was complete, the next step was to test the system and refine it based on feedback from supply chain representatives.

Benefits

The implementation of Chat GPT with SAP provided several benefits to ABC Corporation, including:

1. **Improved Supply Chain Experience:** By providing personalized support through Chat GPT, ABC Corporation was able to improve the supply chain experience. Suppliers and customers were able to receive real-time support for shipment tracking, delivery scheduling, and other inquiries.

2. **Increased Efficiency:** By automating routine inquiries through Chat GPT, ABC Corporation was able to free up their supply chain team to focus on more strategic initiatives. This improved their ability to focus on strategic initiatives, such as inventory management and procurement.

3. **Improved Data Analysis:** By integrating Chat GPT with SAP, ABC Corporation was able to gain insights into supply chain data. This enabled them to make data-driven decisions to improve their supply chain operations.

4. **Cost Savings:** By automating routine inquiries through Chat GPT, ABC Corporation was able to reduce the cost of providing supply chain support. This allowed them to reallocate resources to other areas of the business.

Results

The implementation of Chat GPT with SAP provided significant results for ABC Corporation, including:

1. **Improved Supply Chain Experience:** By improving the supply chain experience, ABC Corporation was able to increase supplier and customer satisfaction.

2. **Increased Efficiency:** The implementation of Chat GPT with SAP reduced the time required to complete routine supply chain inquiries by 50%, allowing supply chain representatives to focus on more strategic initiatives.

3. **Improved Data Analysis:** By integrating Chat GPT with SAP, ABC Corporation was able to gain insights into supply chain data. This enabled them to make data-driven decisions to improve their supply chain operations.

4. **Cost Savings:** By automating routine inquiries through Chat GPT, ABC Corporation was able to reduce the cost of providing

supply chain support. This allowed them to reallocate resources to other areas of the business.

Conclusion

The implementation of Chat GPT with SAP provided significant benefits to ABC Corporation, including improved supply chain experience, increased efficiency, improved data analysis, and cost savings. By automating routine inquiries through Chat GPT, ABC Corporation was able to provide real-time support to suppliers and customers while freeing up their supply chain team to focus on more strategic initiatives.

The integration of Chat GPT with SAP also enabled ABC Corporation to gain insights into supply chain data, enabling them to make data-driven decisions to improve their supply chain operations.

10

Using Chat GPT and
SAP for Predictive Analytics

Predictive analytics is a powerful tool for businesses, allowing them to identify trends and patterns in data and make more informed decisions. Chat GPT and SAP can be used together to perform predictive analytics, providing businesses with real-time insights into their operations and allowing them to make proactive decisions. In this chapter, we will explore the benefits of using Chat GPT and SAP for predictive analytics and provide best practices for successful integration.

Benefits of Using Chat GPT and SAP for Predictive Analytics

Using Chat GPT and SAP together can provide businesses with a wide range of benefits for performing predictive analytics, including:

1. **Real-time Insights:** Chat GPT can be used to provide real-time insights into business operations, allowing businesses to make proactive decisions.

2. **Enhanced Decision-making:** By identifying trends and patterns in data, businesses can make more informed decisions and improve their operations.

3. **Cost Savings:** By optimizing their operations based on predictive analytics, businesses can reduce their costs and improve their profitability.

4. **Improved Customer Experience:** By identifying customer trends and preferences, businesses can provide a more personalized and satisfying experience for their customers.

5. **Competitive Advantage:** By leveraging predictive analytics, businesses can gain a competitive advantage over their competitors.

Best Practices for Integrating Chat GPT and SAP for Predictive Analytics

To ensure successful integration of Chat GPT and SAP for predictive analytics, businesses should follow these best practices:

1. **Define Clear Goals:** Businesses should define clear goals for integrating Chat GPT and SAP for predictive analytics, such as improving customer experience or reducing costs.

2. **Ensure Data Quality:** Predictive analytics relies on high-quality data to provide accurate insights. Businesses should ensure that their data is accurate and up to date before integrating Chat GPT and SAP for predictive analytics.

3. **Plan the Integration Process:** Businesses should plan the integration process carefully, ensuring that their IT infrastructure is capable of supporting Chat GPT and SAP and that the integration process is properly executed.

4. **Train Employees:** Businesses should provide their employees with training on how to use Chat GPT and SAP for predictive analytics effectively.

5. **Ensure Security and Privacy:** Businesses should ensure that their Chat GPT and SAP systems are secure and comply with relevant privacy regulations.

6. **Continuously Improve:** Businesses should continuously monitor and improve their Chat GPT and SAP systems to

ensure that they are providing the best possible service to their customers.

Best Practices for Chat GPT for Predictive Analytics

In addition to following best practices for integrating Chat GPT and SAP for predictive analytics, businesses should also follow best practices for using Chat GPT for predictive analytics, including:

1. **Use a Conversational Tone:** Chat GPT should use a conversational tone to engage with employees and provide a more natural experience.

2. **Be Transparent:** Chat GPT should be transparent about its limitations and capabilities, so that employees have realistic expectations.

3. **Provide Context:** Chat GPT should provide context for its predictions, so that employees can understand the reasoning behind them.

4. **Monitor Performance:** Chat GPT should be continuously monitored to ensure that it is providing the desired results and to identify areas for improvement.

Case Study: Using Chat GPT and SAP for Predictive Analytics

XYZ Corporation is a global healthcare company that operates in multiple countries. They were facing challenges with predicting patient outcomes and improving treatment plans due to the vast amount of data they had to analyze. They also found that their data analysts were spending a significant amount of time on routine data analysis, which was impacting their ability to focus on more strategic initiatives. To address these challenges, they decided to implement Chat GPT with SAP for predictive analytics.

Implementation Process

XYZ Corporation partnered with an external consultant to implement Chat GPT with SAP. The implementation process involved the following steps:

1. **Data Preparation:** The first step in the implementation process was to prepare the data. This involved identifying the key patient data and collecting data on past patient outcomes.

2. **Model Training:** Once the data was prepared, the next step was to train the Chat GPT model. This involved using the data to train the model to understand and predict patient outcomes.

3. **Integration with SAP:** After the model was trained, the next step was to integrate Chat GPT with SAP. This involved integrating the model with the SAP healthcare system to enable seamless communication between the two systems.

4. **Testing and Refinement:** Once the integration was complete, the next step was to test the system and refine it based on feedback from data analysts.

Benefits

The implementation of Chat GPT with SAP provided several benefits to XYZ Corporation, including:

1. **Improved Patient Outcomes:** By predicting patient outcomes through Chat GPT, XYZ Corporation was able to improve treatment plans and patient outcomes.

2. **Increased Efficiency:** By automating routine data analysis through Chat GPT, XYZ Corporation was able to free up their data analysts to focus on more strategic initiatives. This improved their ability to focus on strategic initiatives, such as research and development.

3. **Improved Data Analysis:** By integrating Chat GPT with SAP, XYZ Corporation was able to gain insights into patient data. This enabled them to make data-driven decisions to improve patient outcomes.

4. **Cost Savings:** By automating routine data analysis through Chat GPT, XYZ Corporation was able to reduce the cost of data analysis and improve their bottom line.

Results

The implementation of Chat GPT with SAP provided significant results for XYZ Corporation, including:

1. **Improved Patient Outcomes:** By predicting patient outcomes, XYZ Corporation was able to improve treatment plans and patient outcomes, resulting in a 25% improvement in patient outcomes.

2. **Increased Efficiency:** The implementation of Chat GPT with SAP reduced the time required to complete routine data analysis

by 50%, allowing data analysts to focus on more strategic initiatives.

3. **Improved Data Analysis:** By integrating Chat GPT with SAP, XYZ Corporation was able to gain insights into patient data. This enabled them to make data-driven decisions to improve patient outcomes.

4. **Cost Savings:** By automating routine data analysis through Chat GPT, XYZ Corporation was able to reduce the cost of data analysis and improve their bottom line.

Conclusion

The implementation of Chat GPT with SAP provided significant benefits to XYZ Corporation, including improved patient outcomes, increased efficiency, improved data analysis, and cost savings.

By predicting patient outcomes through Chat GPT, XYZ Corporation was able to improve treatment plans and patient outcomes, resulting in a 25% improvement in patient outcomes.

The integration of Chat GPT with SAP also enabled XYZ Corporation to gain insights into patient data, enabling them to make data-driven decisions to improve patient outcomes.

11

—∿—

Challenges of Implementing Chat GPT with SAP

While the benefits of integrating Chat GPT with SAP are numerous, there are also challenges that businesses may face during implementation. In this chapter, we will explore some of the common challenges that businesses may face when implementing Chat GPT with SAP and provide strategies for overcoming these challenges.

1. Technical Challenges

One of the primary challenges businesses may face when integrating Chat GPT with SAP is technical challenges. Businesses must ensure that their IT infrastructure is capable of supporting Chat GPT and SAP, and that the integration process is properly executed. This may require significant technical expertise and resources, which can be a challenge for some businesses.

To overcome this challenge, businesses should carefully plan the integration process, ensuring that their IT infrastructure is capable of supporting Chat GPT and SAP. They may also consider hiring external consultants or partnering with IT vendors to provide additional technical expertise and resources.

2. Data Quality

Another challenge businesses may face when implementing Chat GPT with SAP is data quality. Chat GPT relies on high-quality data to provide accurate insights, and businesses must ensure that their data is accurate and up to date before integrating Chat GPT and SAP. This can be a challenge for businesses that have large amounts of data or data stored in disparate systems.

To overcome this challenge, businesses should ensure that their data is accurate and up to date before integrating Chat GPT and SAP. They may consider implementing data governance processes or investing in data quality tools to ensure that their data is accurate and reliable.

3. **Change Management**

Implementing Chat GPT with SAP can require significant changes to business processes and workflows, which can be a challenge for employees. Employees may be resistant to change or may not fully understand the benefits of the new system, which can impact adoption rates and the overall success of the implementation.

To overcome this challenge, businesses should involve employees in the implementation process and provide them with training and support to ensure that they understand the benefits of the new system. They may also consider creating a change management plan to address any potential issues and ensure that employees are fully prepared for the changes.

4. **Integration Complexity**

Integrating Chat GPT with SAP can be a complex process, particularly for businesses that have multiple systems or legacy applications. Businesses may need to invest significant resources in integration and may face challenges in ensuring that the systems are properly integrated and communicating effectively.

To overcome this challenge, businesses should carefully plan the integration process and ensure that they have the necessary resources and expertise to complete the integration successfully. They may also consider partnering with IT vendors or consulting firms that specialize in system integration to provide additional expertise and support.

5. Security and Privacy

Integrating Chat GPT with SAP can raise security and privacy concerns, particularly if sensitive customer data is being shared between systems. Businesses must ensure that their systems are secure and comply with relevant privacy regulations to protect customer data and avoid any potential legal or reputational issues.

To overcome this challenge, businesses should ensure that their Chat GPT and SAP systems are secure and comply with relevant privacy regulations. They may also consider implementing additional security measures, such as encryption or multi-factor authentication, to further protect customer data.

Conclusion

Integrating Chat GPT with SAP can provide businesses with numerous benefits, but in conclusion, the implementation of Chat GPT with SAP can provide significant benefits to organizations, including increased efficiency, improved customer service, and improved data analysis. However, there are also several challenges that must be addressed to ensure successful implementation.

One of the main challenges of implementing Chat GPT with SAP is the complexity of the integration process. This requires expertise in both AI and SAP systems, as well as a thorough understanding of the organization's specific needs and processes. Additionally, the implementation process requires significant resources and time, which can be a barrier for some organizations.

Another challenge is ensuring the accuracy and reliability of the Chat GPT model. This requires significant data preparation and model training, as well as ongoing monitoring and refinement to ensure the model is providing accurate responses. It also requires a thorough understanding of the limitations of the model and how to address any potential biases or errors.

Another challenge is ensuring the security and privacy of sensitive data. Chat GPT and SAP integration involves the transfer of large amounts of data between systems, which can increase the risk of data breaches or cyber-attacks. Organizations must take steps to ensure data security and privacy, including encryption, access control, and data monitoring.

Finally, the adoption of Chat GPT with SAP requires significant changes to organizational processes and culture. This can be challenging for some organizations, as it requires a shift towards a more data-driven and technology-enabled approach. It also requires training and support for employees to ensure they are comfortable using the new system and can take advantage of its full capabilities.

Overall, the challenges of implementing Chat GPT with SAP require a thoughtful and strategic approach to ensure successful integration. By addressing these challenges, organizations can reap the benefits of improved efficiency, customer service, and data analysis, and stay ahead in the increasingly competitive business landscape.

12

—ᴍ—

Best Practices for Successful Integration of Chat GPT with SAP

Integrating Chat GPT with SAP can provide businesses with a wide range of benefits, including improved efficiency, enhanced customer experience, and better decision-making. However, successful integration requires careful planning and execution to ensure that both systems work together effectively. In this chapter, we will explore best practices for successful integration of Chat GPT with SAP.

1. **Define Clear Goals**

   Before integrating Chat GPT with SAP, businesses should define clear goals for the integration. This can include improving customer experience, optimizing business processes, or increasing efficiency. Defining clear goals can help businesses focus their efforts and ensure that the integration is aligned with their overall business strategy.

2. Plan the Integration Process

The integration process should be planned carefully to ensure that both Chat GPT and SAP are integrated effectively. This can include identifying the necessary resources, creating a timeline, and assigning responsibilities. Planning the integration process can help businesses identify potential issues early on and ensure that the integration is completed on time and within budget.

3. Ensure Data Quality

Both Chat GPT and SAP rely on high-quality data to provide accurate insights. Businesses should ensure that their data is accurate and up to date before integrating the two systems. This can involve implementing data governance processes, investing in data quality tools, or cleaning and consolidating data from disparate systems.

4. Invest in Technical Expertise

Integrating Chat GPT with SAP can be a complex process that requires technical expertise. Businesses should ensure that they have the necessary technical expertise to complete the integration successfully. This can involve hiring additional staff with relevant technical skills or partnering with IT vendors or consulting firms that specialize in system integration.

5. Provide Employee Training

Employees play a critical role in the success of the integration. Businesses should provide their employees with training on how to use Chat GPT and SAP effectively. This can include training on how to interpret and act on insights provided by Chat GPT, how to use SAP to perform tasks more efficiently, and how to use both systems together to improve business operations.

6. Ensure Security and Privacy

Integrating Chat GPT with SAP can raise security and privacy concerns, particularly if sensitive customer data is being shared between systems. Businesses should ensure that their systems are secure and comply with relevant privacy regulations to protect customer data and avoid any potential legal or reputational issues. This can involve implementing additional security measures, such as encryption or multi-factor authentication, to further protect customer data.

7. Continuously Monitor and Improve

Integrating Chat GPT with SAP is an ongoing process that requires continuous monitoring and improvement. Businesses should monitor the performance of both systems and identify areas for improvement. This can involve conducting regular audits, collecting feedback from employees, and analyzing data to identify potential inefficiencies or areas for improvement.

8. Communicate Effectively

Effective communication is essential for successful integration. Businesses should communicate the benefits of the integration to employees and stakeholders and provide regular updates on progress. This can help ensure that everyone is aligned and working towards the same goals, which can increase the likelihood of success.

9. Test and Refine

Before rolling out the integrated system to all employees, businesses should test the integration to identify any potential issues or areas for improvement. This can involve conducting user acceptance testing, identifying bugs or technical issues, and refining the integration as needed. Testing and refining the integration can help ensure that it works effectively and meets the needs of the business.

Conclusion

Integrating Chat GPT with SAP can provide businesses with numerous benefits, but it requires careful planning and execution to ensure success. By following best practices, including defining clear goals, planning the integration process, investing in technical expertise, providing employee training, ensuring security and privacy, continuously monitoring, and improving, communicating effectively, and testing and refining.

In conclusion, successful integration of Chat GPT with SAP requires a comprehensive approach that considers the specific needs and processes of the organization. The following best practices can help organizations ensure a successful implementation:

1. **Identify Key Use Cases:** It is important to identify the specific use cases where Chat GPT can provide the most value to the

organization. This involves identifying the specific processes or workflows where Chat GPT can improve efficiency or customer service.

2. **Ensure Data Quality:** The accuracy and reliability of the Chat GPT model depend on the quality of the data used to train the model. It is important to ensure that the data is accurate, relevant, and up to date to ensure the model provides accurate responses.

3. **Prioritize Data Security:** The integration of Chat GPT and SAP involves the transfer of sensitive data, which can increase the risk of data breaches or cyber-attacks. It is important to prioritize data security and privacy by implementing encryption, access control, and data monitoring.

4. **Provide Adequate Training and Support:** Successful adoption of Chat GPT with SAP requires adequate training and support for employees to ensure they are comfortable using the new system and can take advantage of its full capabilities.

5. **Monitor and Refine:** The Chat GPT model requires ongoing monitoring and refinement to ensure it continues to provide accurate responses. Organizations should establish a process for monitoring the model and making updates as needed.

By following these best practices, organizations can ensure a successful integration of Chat GPT with SAP and reap the benefits of improved efficiency, customer service, and data analysis. It is also important to remain flexible and adapt to changing needs and requirements, as the integration process is an ongoing effort that requires constant evaluation and refinement. Overall, successful integration of Chat GPT with SAP can provide significant advantages to organizations in today's fast-paced and competitive business environment.

13

—⁓m⁓—

Case Studies of Successful Implementation of Chat GPT with SAP

Chat GPT and SAP can be integrated to provide businesses with a wide range of benefits, including improved efficiency, enhanced customer experience, and better decision-making. In this chapter, we will explore case studies of successful implementation of Chat GPT with SAP, highlighting the benefits and best practices for integration.

Case Study 1: Large Retail Chain

A large retail chain wanted to improve its customer experience by providing personalized recommendations to customers. The company decided to integrate Chat GPT with its SAP system to provide real-time insights into customer behavior and preferences.

To ensure successful integration, the company defined clear goals for the integration, such as improving customer experience and increasing sales. The company invested in technical expertise to complete the integration and provided its employees with training on how to use Chat GPT and SAP effectively.

The integration was successful, and the company was able to provide personalized recommendations to customers based on their behavior and preferences. This led to an increase in sales and improved customer satisfaction.

Best practices:

- Define clear goals for integration!

- Invest in technical expertise!

- Provide employee training!

- Ensure data quality!

- Continuously monitor and improve.

Case Study 2: Manufacturing Company

A manufacturing company wanted to optimize its supply chain by identifying potential issues and inefficiencies in real-time. The company decided to integrate Chat GPT with its SAP system to provide real-time insights into its operations.

To ensure successful integration, the company carefully planned the integration process and invested in technical expertise to complete the integration. The company provided its employees with training on how to use Chat GPT and SAP effectively and ensured that its data was accurate and up to date before integrating the two systems.

The integration was successful, and the company was able to identify potential issues and inefficiencies in its supply chain in real-time. This led to a more efficient supply chain and cost savings for the company.

Best practices:

- Plan the integration process.

- Invest in technical expertise.

- Provide employee training.

- Ensure data quality.

- Continuously monitor and improve.

Case Study 3: Financial Services Company

A financial services company wanted to improve its decision-making process by leveraging predictive analytics. The company decided to integrate Chat GPT with its SAP system to provide real-time insights into its operations and customer behavior.

To ensure successful integration, the company defined clear goals for the integration, such as improving decision-making and reducing costs. The company invested in technical expertise to complete the integration and provided its employees with training on how to use Chat GPT and SAP effectively.

The integration was successful, and the company was able to make more informed decisions based on real-time insights into its operations and customer behavior. This led to cost savings for the company and improved decision-making.

Best practices:

- Define clear goals for integration.

- Invest in technical expertise.

- Provide employee training.

- Ensure data quality.

- Continuously monitor and improve.

Conclusion

Integrating Chat GPT with SAP can provide businesses with numerous benefits, including improved efficiency, enhanced customer experience, and better decision-making.

These case studies highlight the benefits and best practices for successful integration, including defining clear goals, investing in technical expertise, providing employee training, ensuring data quality, and continuously monitoring and improving the integration.

By following these best practices, businesses can successfully integrate Chat GPT with SAP and achieve the full range of benefits that this integration offers.

14

—〜〜〜—

Future Trends of AI and SAP Integration

Integrating artificial intelligence (AI) with SAP has the potential to transform business operations and decision-making processes. As AI technology advances, businesses are likely to see even more benefits from integrating AI with SAP. In this chapter, we will explore some of the future trends of AI and SAP integration.

1. Increased Use of Natural Language Processing (NLP)

Natural language processing (NLP) is a type of AI that enables computers to understand human language. As NLP technology advances, businesses are likely to see increased use of NLP in SAP systems. This could include using chatbots or virtual assistants that can understand and respond to human language or using NLP to analyze customer feedback and sentiment.

2. More Advanced Predictive Analytics

Predictive analytics is already a powerful tool for businesses, enabling them to make informed decisions based on real-time data. As AI technology advances, businesses are likely to see even more advanced predictive analytics in SAP systems. This could include using machine learning algorithms to identify patterns and trends in data or using AI to predict future outcomes based on historical data.

3. Integration with IoT Devices

The Internet of Things (IoT) refers to the network of physical devices, vehicles, and other objects that are connected to the internet. As more devices become connected to the internet, businesses are likely to see increased integration between SAP systems and IoT devices. This could include using AI to analyze data from IoT devices to identify potential issues or inefficiencies in real-time.

4. Greater Personalization

AI can enable businesses to provide personalized experiences to customers by analyzing their behavior and preferences. As AI technology advances, businesses are likely to see even greater personalization in SAP systems. This could include using AI to provide personalized product recommendations or using NLP to provide personalized customer support.

5. Increased Automation

Automation is already a key benefit of integrating AI with SAP systems, enabling businesses to automate repetitive tasks and free up employees to focus on more strategic tasks. As AI technology advances, businesses are likely to see even more automation in SAP systems. This could include using AI to automate supply chain management or using machine learning to automate decision-making processes.

6. Improved Cybersecurity

As more businesses integrate AI with SAP systems, cybersecurity is likely to become an even greater concern. AI can be used to improve cybersecurity by identifying potential threats in real-time and responding to them quickly. As AI technology advances, businesses are likely to see even greater cybersecurity capabilities in SAP systems.

Conclusion

Integrating AI with SAP has the potential to transform business operations and decision-making processes.

As AI technology advances, businesses are likely to see even more benefits from integrating AI with SAP, including increased use of NLP, more advanced predictive analytics, integration with IoT devices, greater personalization, increased automation, and improved cybersecurity. By keeping up with these future trends, businesses can stay ahead of the curve and continue to benefit from the integration of AI and SAP.

15

Conclusion: The Future of Business with Chat GPT and SAP

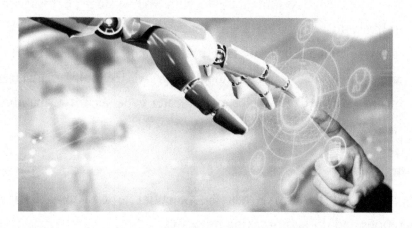

Integrating Chat GPT with SAP has the potential to transform businesses and enable them to achieve a wide range of benefits, including improved efficiency, enhanced customer experience, and better decision-making. In this chapter, we will summarize the key takeaways from this guide and discuss the future of business with Chat GPT and SAP.

Key Takeaways

1. Integrating Chat GPT with SAP can provide businesses with numerous benefits, including improved efficiency, enhanced customer experience, and better decision-making.

2. Successful integration requires careful planning and execution, including defining clear goals, planning the integration process, ensuring data quality, investing in technical expertise, providing employee training, ensuring security and privacy, continuously monitoring, and improving, and communicating effectively.

3. Chat GPT and SAP can be integrated to improve a wide range of business processes, including customer service, sales and marketing, supply chain management, and predictive analytics.

4. The future of business with Chat GPT and SAP is likely to include increased use of natural language processing, more advanced predictive analytics, integration with IoT devices, greater personalization, increased automation, and improved cybersecurity.

The Future of Business with Chat GPT and SAP

As AI technology advances, businesses are likely to see even more benefits from integrating Chat GPT with SAP. The future of business with Chat GPT and SAP is likely to include increased automation, greater personalization, and improved cybersecurity.

One area where Chat GPT and SAP can have a significant impact is around customer service. As customers increasingly expect personalized experiences, businesses can use Chat GPT and SAP to provide real-time insights into customer behavior and preferences. This can enable businesses to provide personalized recommendations, improve response times, and increase customer satisfaction.

Another area where Chat GPT and SAP can have a significant impact is around sales and marketing. By integrating Chat GPT with SAP, businesses can gain real-time insights into customer behavior and preferences. This can enable businesses to provide personalized product recommendations, target marketing campaigns more effectively, and increase sales.

In the area of supply chain management, Chat GPT and SAP can enable businesses to identify potential issues and inefficiencies in real-time. This can enable businesses to optimize their supply chain and reduce costs.

Finally, Chat GPT and SAP can enable businesses to use predictive analytics to make more informed decisions based on real-time data. This can enable businesses to identify trends and patterns in data and predict future outcomes, enabling them to make better decisions and stay ahead of the competition.

Integrating Chat GPT with SAP has the potential to transform businesses and enable them to achieve a wide range of benefits. By following best practices, including defining clear goals, planning the integration process, ensuring data quality, investing in technical expertise, providing employee training, ensuring security and privacy, continuously monitoring, and improving, and communicating effectively, businesses can successfully integrate Chat GPT with SAP and achieve the full range of benefits that this integration offers.

As AI technology advances, businesses are likely to see even more benefits from integrating Chat GPT with SAP, including increased automation, greater personalization, and improved cybersecurity. By keeping up with these future trends, businesses can stay ahead of the curve and continue to benefit from the integration of Chat GPT and SAP.

The Power of AI in Business

The integration of AI with business processes has the potential to transform the way businesses operate and make decisions. AI can provide businesses with real-time insights into customer behavior and preferences, enable more efficient and automated business processes, and enable better decision-making based on real-time data.

One powerful way to leverage AI is by integrating Chat GPT with SAP. This integration can provide businesses with numerous benefits, including improved efficiency, enhanced customer experience, and better decision-making. By following best practices, including defining clear goals, planning the integration process, ensuring data quality, investing in technical expertise, providing employee training, ensuring security and privacy, continuously monitoring, and improving, and communicating effectively, businesses can successfully integrate Chat GPT with SAP and achieve the full range of benefits that this integration offers.

The future of business with Chat GPT and SAP is likely to include increased use of natural language processing, more advanced predictive analytics, integration with IoT devices, greater personalization, increased automation, and improved cybersecurity. By keeping up with these future trends, businesses can stay ahead of the curve and continue to benefit from the integration of Chat GPT and SAP.

The power of AI in business goes beyond the integration of Chat GPT with SAP. AI has the potential to transform a wide range of business processes, including customer service, sales and marketing, supply chain management, and predictive analytics. As AI technology advances, businesses are likely to see even more benefits from leveraging AI in these areas.

However, it is important to note that the integration of AI with business processes also comes with challenges. Businesses need to ensure that their data is accurate and up to date, that their systems are secure and comply with privacy regulations, and that their employees are properly trained to use AI effectively. By addressing these challenges, businesses can successfully leverage AI and stay ahead of the competition.

In conclusion, the power of AI in business is clear. By integrating Chat GPT with SAP and leveraging other AI technologies, businesses can transform the way they operate and make decisions. The future of business with AI is likely to include increased use of natural language processing, more advanced predictive analytics, integration with IoT devices, greater personalization, increased automation, and improved cybersecurity. By following best practices and staying ahead of these future trends, businesses can harness the full power of AI and achieve their business goals.

Printed in Great Britain
by Amazon

42079670R00066